Big Machines

CRANES

I0821805

By Katie Kawa

Please visit our website, www.garethstevens.com. For a free color catalog of all our high-quality books, call toll free 1-800-542-2595 or fax 1-877-542-2596.

Library of Congress Cataloging-in-Publication Data

Kawa, Katie.
Cranes / Katie Kawa.
p. cm. — (Big machines)
Includes index.
ISBN 978-1-4339-5556-3 (pbk.)
ISBN 978-1-4339-5557-0 (6-pack)
ISBN 978-1-4339-5554-9 (library binding)
1. Cranes, derricks, etc.—Juvenile literature. I. Title.
TJ1363.K377 2011
621.8'73—dc22
2011006574

First Edition

Published in 2012 by
Gareth Stevens Publishing
111 East 14th Street, Suite 349
New York, NY 10003

Editor: Katie Kawa
Designer: Daniel Hosek

Photo credits: Cover, p. 1 Thinkstock.com; pp. 5, 7, 9, 11, 13, 19, 21, 23 Shutterstock.com; pp. 15, 17 iStockphoto.com.

Printed in the United States of America

CPSIA compliance information: Batch #CS11GS: For further information contact Gareth Stevens, New York, New York at 1-800-542-2595.

Contents

Cranes pull things up.

Cranes carry big things.

S.W.L.
35.000 KG

A crane has a hook.
The hook pulls things.

A crane has a kind of arm. It is called a boom.

Cranes move on trucks.

A sky crane can fly!

Sky cranes carry trees.

A tower crane is a tall crane. It is too tall to move.

It carries tools.

Cranes work in the city!

Words to Know

boom

hook

Index